Prentice Hall's Reality Reading Series

Juvenile Justice
A Collection
of True-Crime Cases

RON GRIMMING

Director of Miami Dade College, School of Justice (Retired)
Director of the Florida Highway Patrol (Retired)
Deputy Director of the Illinois State Police (Retired)

DEBBIE J. GOODMAN, M.S.

Chairperson of Miami Dade College, School of Justice

PEARSON
Prentice
Hall

Upper Saddle River, New Jersey 07458

Library of Congress Cataloging-in-Publication Data

Grimming, Ron.
  Juvenile justice : a collection of true-crime cases / Ron Grimming, Debbie J. Goodman.
    p. cm. — (Prentice Hall's reality reading series)
  ISBN-13: 978-0-13-512782-7 (alk. paper)
  ISBN-10: 0-13-512782-3
  1. Juvenile homicide—United States—Case studies. 2. Juvenile homicide—Great Britain—Case studies. 3. Violence in children—United States—Case studies. 4. Violence in children—Great Britain—Case studies. I. Goodman, Debbie J. II. Title.
  HV9067.H6G75 2007
  364.152'3092273—dc22

                                                    2007029391

Editor-in-Chief: Vernon R. Anthony
Senior Acquisitions Editor: Tim Peyton
Editorial Assistant: Alicia Kelly
Marketing Manager: Adam Kloza
Production Liaison: Joanne Riker
Cover Design Director: Jayne Conte
Cover Design: Karen Salzbach
Full-Service Project Management/Composition: Karpagam Jagadeesan/ GGS Book Services

Credits and acknowledgments borrowed from other sources and reproduced, with permission, in this textbook appear on appropriate page within text.

Pearson Education LTD.
Pearson Education Australia PTY, Limited
Pearson Education Singapore, Pte. Ltd
Pearson Education North Asia Ltd
Pearson Education, Canada, Ltd
Pearson Educación de Mexico, S.A. de C.V.
Pearson Education–Japan
Pearson Education Malaysia, Pte. Ltd

ISBN-13: 978-0-13-512782-7
ISBN-10:   0-13-512782-3

From Ron Grimming

To Karen, I thank you for your support, your understanding, and your love!

and

To the men and women who aspire to become members of the criminal justice profession, I encourage you to dream your dream and then make it happen.

From Debbie J. Goodman

To Glenn, Connor, and Carson, my heroes, I love you more than words can express.

and

To the past, present, and future criminal justice professionals, thank you for your exemplary service to our communities.

Contents

Preface

Criminal behavior is a phenomenon, a daily unwanted reality, that angers, intrigues, puzzles, and plagues most members of society, particularly law enforcement officials, politicians, teachers, clergy, parents, medical professionals, and the elderly, to name a few.

When juveniles commit violent acts of crime, especially murder, several questions come to mind:

- Who are these kids?
- Why do they commit crime?
- How should society handle them?
- Should they be punished or treated?
- Should juveniles receive the death penalty?
- Should parents be held accountable for the violent actions of their kids?

These poignant questions and many others are presented in *Juvenile Justice: A Collection of True-Crime Cases,* which is the second book in Prentice Hall's 10-part Reality Reading Series. The book is designed to encourage vibrant discussion in college and university settings among professors and students alike. Its purpose is to present a dose of reality—chilling and thrilling true-crime cases of violent kids and the crimes they've perpetrated. The authors, who combined have more than 50 years of experience as criminal justice practitioners and educators, anticipate lively debate and encourage students to actively participate in the section titled "You're the Investigator" at the conclusion of each case.

Although juvenile crime and violence will not disappear, it is through this book and other criminal justice texts that criminologists, psychologists, academicians, and students can perhaps reach a level of understanding about this disruptive social condition.

Juvenile Justice: A Collection of True-Crime Cases is recommended for academic use as a supplemental text for college and university juvenile justice/juvenile delinquency courses. It is not designed to be as comprehensive as a primary text; rather, it provides a brief overview of key topics for the students' review and focuses on real-life cases for students to analyze.

Enjoy Book II of the Reality Reading Series and the stimulating dialogue and discussion that will be generated during classroom interaction.

Best regards,
Ron Grimming
Debbie J. Goodman

Acknowledgments

The authors gratefully acknowledge the students, faculty, staff, and administrators at Miami Dade College in Miami, Florida, for their support.

A special thanks to the talented experts at Prentice Hall Publishing: Robin Baliszewski, Tim Peyton, Sarah Holle, and Adam Kloza.

Thank you, Mary Greene, for your wonderful expertise involving manuscript coordination.

A special thanks to Joanne Riker at Prentice Hall and Karpagam Jagadeesan at GGS Book Services.

About the Authors

Ron Grimming

Ron Grimming has an extensive and impressive 33-year background in law enforcement. His career in law enforcement began in 1970 as a special agent with the Illinois State Police. He served in various investigative assignments, including special task forces targeting criminal activities associated with subversive groups, political and police corruption, illegal drugs, and financial crimes. He was promoted numerous times during his career and attained the rank of deputy director of the Illinois State Police, supervising more than 2,500 officers assigned to the investigative and patrol divisions of the department. In 1993, Grimming was appointed director of the Florida Highway Patrol, where he managed the activities of 1,740 sworn officers and 528 civilian personnel. Grimming focused the patrol's mission on highway safety through traffic enforcement, accident investigation, prevention of highway violence, interdiction of illegal contraband, investigation of auto theft, and the development of public safety education programs. Through Grimming's leadership, the Florida Highway Patrol received the recognition of being nationally accredited by the Commission on Accreditation for Law Enforcement Agencies after having its policies and operational procedures scrutinized by a panel of nationally recognized law enforcement experts. Also, under Grimming's guidance, the patrol won the prestigious National Chief's Challenge, designating it as having the best traffic safety program in the nation. During his law enforcement career, Grimming has served as general chairman of the International Association of Chiefs of Police (IACP), State and Provincial Police Division, which represents the nation's state police and highway patrol organizations on the IACP Board of Directors. Grimming also served as chairman of the IACP Organized Crime Committee and president of the State

Law Enforcement Chief's Association. Grimming has an extensive law enforcement training background, having served on Florida's Criminal Justice Standards and Training Commission. He recently retired as director of Miami Dade College's School of Justice, which has responsibility for college criminal justice degree programs, as well as law enforcement, corrections, and security officer training for Miami-Dade County criminal justice agencies.

Debbie J. Goodman

Debbie J. Goodman, M.S., is the chairperson of the School of Justice at Miami Dade College. She holds a master of science degree in criminal justice from Florida International University and a bachelor of science degree in criminology from Florida State University. Goodman specializes in a wide range of criminal justice topics, including report writing, ethics, communications, human behavior, juvenile justice, criminology, criminal justice, and leadership. She is the author of recognized national publications: *Report It in Writing, Enforcing Ethics, Florida Crime and Justice, The Search and Seizure Handbook, Work in Criminal Justice, and Criminal Justice: Reality Reading Series*. Goodman is an adjunct faculty member in the College of Public Affairs at Florida International University and was honored in 2002 and 2005 by *Who's Who Among America's Teachers* as one of the nation's most talented college instructors. She is committed to providing quality education and training to police and corrections officers as well as criminal justice college students and practitioners. She resides in South Florida with her husband and two sons.

Introduction

Juvenile crime is one of the nation's most serious crime problems. Concern about juvenile crime is widely shared by federal, state, and local law enforcement officials as well as juvenile justice agencies.

Of particular concern is the escalating level of violence being perpetrated by juveniles against both the juvenile and adult populations. As an example, according to 2006 Federal Bureau of Investigation (FBI) data, large numbers of teenage gangs are getting actively involved in committing bank robberies. The FBI has indicated that teenagers are forming large groups to carry out bank robbery schemes. The accused in most of these youth-bank robberies are teens in the age-group of 15 to 17 years old.

In addition, 2006 data collected by the Office of Juvenile Justice and Delinquency Prevention, FBI, World Health Organization, and the Center for Health Statistics provide the following important information when considering key facts about youth violence:

- Violence is the second leading cause of death for young people in America and the leading cause of death for young people in every major city.
- American young people are five to ten times more likely to die from violence than children in any other industrialized nation in the world.
- Juvenile violence and crime rates triple in the hour immediately after school.
- Every year, an average of 3,024 children die in the United States from gunfire.
- Nearly 58,000 juveniles were murdered between 1980 and 2006; one in four involved a juvenile offender, and 77% were killed with a firearm.

- More than one in four identified juvenile murderers in 2006 was located in eight of the nation's more than 3,000 counties. These eight counties contain 12% of the U.S. population.
- One in five juvenile arrestees carried a handgun all or most of the time.
- More than half of all 16-year-olds who ever committed assault, carried a handgun, or belonged to a gang had done so for the first time by age 12.
- Fewer than half of serious violent crimes committed by juveniles are reported to law enforcement.
- The direct and indirect costs to Americans of violent crimes and crimes involving property are $425 billion each year.
- In 2006, most states around the country spent more money building prisons than colleges.

CHAPTER 1

Juvenile Justice: A Glimpse at Reality

The reality, ladies and gentlemen, is that young people have choices. Many choose a path of law-abiding conduct, whereas others choose a path of lawlessness. Some will go to prestigious colleges and universities such as Penn State, whereas others will go to the State Pen! So, who are these kids, why do they do what they do, what influences them, and what can and should society do about it?

In this chapter, we want to motivate you to analyze these issues and discuss key points with your fellow classmates and professors.

Let's take a look.

A Glimpse at Reality: Who are Today's Juvenile Offenders?

According to 2006 Bureau of Justice Statistics (BJS) pertaining to incarcerated youth throughout the United States, the following facts provide a picture of today's youthful offender:

- 87% of incarcerated youth are male.
- 40% are black.

- 38% are Anglo/white.
- 19% are Hispanic.
- 3% are comprised of other ethnic categories.
- 89% admitted to frequent drug and/or alcohol usage.
- 86% experienced early school detachment (i.e., truancy, poor grades, behavioral issues, failure of one or more grade levels).
- 79% dropped out of school prior to high school graduation.
- 68% admitted to involvement in gang activity.
- 61% live in a one-parent household.
- 47% have an older sibling or relative who is involved in criminal activity.
- 10% of juvenile arrestees are under the age of 12.
- 4% have contemplated suicide.

Relevant Terms

Delinquency is defined as conduct that violates criminal law, juvenile status offenses, and other juvenile misconduct.

A *delinquent* is a juvenile who has committed a delinquent act. The term is applied to children to avoid stigmatizing these individuals with the term *criminal.*

A *gang* is a group of three or more persons whose primary focus is participating in criminal conduct together.

Status offenses are activities or conduct, considered offenses, when committed by juveniles. Common activities in this category include buying alcohol, being truant from school, purchasing cigarettes, running away from home, and incorrigibility (being out of control).

Why Do They Do It?

This is a critical question that has plagued, puzzled, and intrigued criminologists, psychologists, teachers, parents, politicians, law enforcement officials and citizens for years.

Recent surveys and studies of juvenile offenders conducted by the National Institute of Justice (NIJ) offer the following ten rationales:

1. Money
2. Revenge/anger
3. Fun
4. Easy to get away with it
5. Boredom
6. Peer pressure
7. Drugs (under the influence of a substance during the commission of a crime)
8. Opportunity exists
9. Frustration
10. Alienation from school (feeling apart from rather than a part of the mainstream crowd)

Class activity: List five more reasons why you believe juveniles commit crime.

1. _____
2. _____
3. _____
4. _____
5. _____

Punishment versus Rehabilitation?

This is a key issue that has been debated for years and will continue to be argued for many years to come. Historically, juvenile court judges have tried to "help" the youthful offender. The question today is, *Should juveniles be punished for the crime they committed, or should they be treated in hopes that they can be rehabilitated?*

Class activity: Discuss this issue with your classmates and professor. Provide five points that support the punishment of juveniles and five points that support the rehabilitation of juveniles.

Pro	Con
1. _____	1. _____
2. _____	2. _____
3. _____	3. _____
4. _____	4. _____
5. _____	5. _____

A second controversial issue for your consideration is that of the death penalty. Discuss with your classmates and professor whether you believe juveniles should be sentenced to death for committing heinous crimes or whether they should be spared such a sentence because of their age and lack of maturity.

Pro	Con
1. _____	1. _____
2. _____	2. _____
3. _____	3. _____
4. _____	4. _____
5. _____	5. _____

A third issue of significance for class discussion is that of holding parents liable for the delinquent actions of their children. Do you think mom or dad should be held accountable if their son or daughter is "out of control" and breaks the law? Discuss with your classmates and professor. Provide five supporting points for each side.

Pro	Con
1. _____	1. _____
2. _____	2. _____
3. _____	3. _____
4. _____	4. _____
5. _____	5. _____

A fourth and final critical issue we would like you to think about is the role the media plays (if any) in encouraging violent behavior among juveniles. One of the most talked about and referenced cases on this topic is the 1977 case of Ronnie Zamora, who, as a 15-year-old in South Florida, was convicted of first-degree murder for killing his elderly neighbor, Elinor Haggart. Zamora's attorney at the time, Ellis Rubin, used an insanity defense termed "television intoxication," suggesting that Zamora's repeated watching of violence on television led to this vicious crime. The defense was not successful, and Zamora was sentenced to life imprisonment.

Do you think today's television programs, movies, music industry, Internet exposure, and so on encourage juvenile violence? Discuss your points in class.

Yes	No
1. _____	1. _____
2. _____	2. _____
3. _____	3. _____
4. _____	4. _____
5. _____	5. _____

Steps in the Juvenile Justice Process

Here is a brief overview, for your review, of how today's juvenile justice system works.

Step 1: *Intake*

A juvenile will enter the system either through an arrest by a police officer or through the filing of a juvenile petition. Petitions are complaints that may be filed by parents, teachers, school administrators, and so on alleging illegal or uncontrollable behavior.

Step 2: *Detention Hearing*

This phase in the process focuses on whether or not the juvenile should be held or detained. The outcome of the hearing can result in a number of different options: detention in a facility; diversion to a drug-treatment program, a counseling service, job training, or a mental health program; or release into the custody of parents.

Step 3: *Preliminary Hearing*

The primary purpose of the preliminary hearing is to determine whether there is probable cause to believe the juvenile committed the act for which he or she is accused. If so, and if probable cause is established, the juvenile may be offered diversionary alternatives. However, if a serious crime is established, the juvenile may be transferred into the adult court system.

Step 4: *Adjudicatory Hearing*

During this stage in the process, which for a juvenile is comparable to an adult trial, there are significant differences, including the following:

   a. *No trial by jury*—Juveniles do not have a constitutional right to a trial by jury (adults do).

   b. *Informal*—Adult trials are highly formal, whereas in the juvenile court setting, the proceedings often appear as conversations.

   c. *Private*—These hearings are not open to scrutiny by the public or media.

d. *Speed*—Juvenile proceedings tend to be completed in a few hours or days, whereas in the adult setting, they could last weeks or months.

e. *Language*—Juveniles may be determined to be "delinquent" rather than "guilty."

Step 5: *Disposition Hearing*

The disposition hearing in juvenile court is similar to the sentencing hearing in adult court. The primary focus is to determine what action should be taken pertaining to the juvenile. Ultimately, the judge's decision involves whether to confine the juvenile. In the majority of matters, judges attempt to provide a sentence that is in the best interest of the juvenile.

Historical Juvenile Justice Cases

To understand the present and future, we need to be reminded of the impact these historical cases have had and continue to have on today's system.

Kent v. U.S. (1966)

Facts: In 1959, in the District of Colombia, Morris Kent Jr., age 14, was apprehended and charged with a home burglary and attempted purse snatching. For these actions, Kent was released into his mother's custody and placed on juvenile probation.

Then, in 1966, Kent was interrogated for entering a woman's apartment, taking her wallet, and raping her. He admitted to committing the crime as well as several other burglaries, robberies, and rapes. Kent was assigned to adult court and indicted on eight counts of burglary, robbery, and rape. Kent's lawyer challenged the transfer into the adult court system and won.

Rule of Law

The Kent case maintained that juveniles should be afforded adequate treatment and consideration before they can be transferred to adult court. Additionally, the Kent case ruled that juveniles are entitled to be represented by attorneys.

In re Gault (1964)

Facts: In 1964, in Arizona, Gerald Gault and Ronald Levin were taken into custody on the basis of a complaint made by their neighbor that the boys made lewd remarks to her via their telephone. A judge adjudicated Gault delinquent for this activity. However, his attorneys appealed the ruling on the basis of their contention that Gault's constitutional rights were violated as a result of a lack of due process being adhered to during the process.

Rule of Law

The Supreme Court ruled in favor of Gault and set the foundation for the following procedural rights to occur in juvenile court settings. A juvenile has a right to the following:

1. Notice of charges against him or her
2. Counsel
3. Confront and cross-examine witnesses
4. Be protected against self-incrimination

In re Winship (1969)

Facts: In the late 1960s, in New York, 12-year-old Samuel Winship was adjudicated delinquent for entering a locker and stealing $112 from a pocketbook. Winship's attorneys appealed on the grounds of the "evidence standard" stating that a "preponderance of the evidence" is inconsistent with "beyond a reasonable doubt."

Rule of Law

As a result of the *Winship* case, the higher court ruled that delinquency must be established "beyond a reasonable doubt."

McKeiver v. Pennsylvania (1971)

Facts: In 1971, in Pennsylvania, 16-year-old Joseph McKeiver was charged with robbery, larceny, and receiving stolen property. He had no prior arrests and was employed at the time. McKeiver's attorney maintained that his client be afforded a jury trial. The court denied this request. His attorney challenged the U.S. Supreme Court on the basis of juveniles being permitted a jury trial.

Rule of Law

The Supreme Court held that the Constitution does not mandate jury trials for juveniles and maintained this position.

Breed v. Jones (1975)

Facts: In 1971, 17-year-old Jones was adjudicated delinquent for the crime of robbery with a deadly weapon. During a later disposition hearing, he was determined to be unfit for juvenile treatment and therefore transferred to a higher court for trial as an adult, where he was found guilty of first-degree robbery. Jones's attorneys appealed to the U.S. Supreme Court on the basis of double jeopardy since he had already been adjudicated in a juvenile court environment.

Rule of Law

The Supreme Court agreed with Jones's attorneys, and he was returned to juvenile court, thereby maintaining that juveniles cannot be subjected to double jeopardy.

Schall v. Martin (1984)

Facts: In 1984, in New York City, 14-year-old Gregory Martin was arrested for robbery and weapon possession. He was detained in a detention facility for more than two weeks awaiting his hearing. Martin was adjudicated delinquent, and his attorneys challenged the U.S. Supreme Court and argued that Martin's detention was a denial of the Fourteenth Amendment.

Rule of Law

The Supreme Court ruled, on the basis of significant risk and to prevent future delinquency, that detention of juveniles does not violate the Fourteenth Amendment's "principle of due process."

New Jersey v. T.L.O. (1985)

Facts: In 1985, a 14-year-old girl in New Jersey was accused of a school-rule violation of smoking in a high school bathroom. The girl, referred to in court documents as T.L.O., was subjected to a search of her purse by a vice principal of the high school. The search resulted in a finding of marijuana in T.L.O.'s purse. T.L.O. was later adjudicated delinquent in court. Her lawyers appealed to the New Jersey Supreme Court on the grounds that a search of T.L.O.'s purse was regarded as an item of personal property and therefore was unreasonable.

Rule of Law

The higher court ruled that school officials are prohibited from engaging in unreasonable searches of students and their property.

Illinois v. Montanez (1996)

Facts: In 1992, in Illinois, 15-year-old Jacqueline Montanez admitted to participating in two execution-style murders of rival gang members who were two boys of the Latin Kings gang. Both boys had been shot at close range in the back of the head. Montanez and two of her fellow female gang members of the Maniac Latin Disciples were arrested. Montanez was charged as an adult. She was advised of her rights to remain silent and to have a lawyer present during questioning. She refused a lawyer and made incriminating statements during the interrogation to police. She was later convicted of two counts of homicide. Her attorneys challenged a higher court on the grounds that her mother was not allowed to be present during her interrogation.

Rule of Law

The Court of Appeals of Illinois ruled that because Montanez made incriminating statements, which ultimately resulted in her confession without her mother being present, the confession should have been suppressed.

CHAPTER 2

The Columbine Tragedy

One of the most violent school tragedies in U.S. history occurred on April 20, 1999, in Littleton, Colorado, when two students, 18-year-old Eric Harris and 17-year-old Dylan Klebold, went on a shooting rampage. Before taking their own lives, Harris and Klebold casually walked through the hallways, classrooms, and cafeteria at Columbine High School, shooting and killing 13 students and faculty and seriously wounding 25 others.

Columbine High School, with an enrollment of more than 1,900 students, is located in Jefferson County, Colorado, which is in the foothills on the west side of the Denver metropolitan area. This usually calm and tranquil region would forever be changed by the violent and brutal behavior of Harris and Klebold.

According to Jefferson County Sheriff's office reports, the two gunmen began developing their plan more than a year before the attack on the school to kill as many students and faculty as possible. Plans recovered by investigators after the shooting further revealed that Harris and Klebold would set off bombs in the school and then shoot students and teachers as they evacuated the school. The shooters also planned to plant explosive devices in their cars, which were timed to explode and kill law enforcement and fire rescue personnel as they arrived at the scene.

Their handwritten notes, later discovered by law enforcement, indicated that Harris and Klebold initially planned the attack on Columbine High School for Monday, April 19, 1999. Although Harris and Klebold's writings made no reference to the historical significance of this date, it should be pointed out that April 19, 1999, was the fourth anniversary of the tragic bombing of the Alfred P. Murrah Federal Building in Oklahoma City and the sixth anniversary of the Branch Davidian assault in Waco, Texas. Why Klebold and Harris waited one day, until April 20, to conduct their rampage is only speculation, but authorities believe that the postponement occurred because of last-minute preparations before the attack.

Attack on Columbine

April 20, 1999, began as an uneventful day at Columbine High School, until about 11:35 A.M., when students heard popping noises coming from outside the cafeteria and believed they were firecrackers being ignited as a part of a senior day prank. Similar pranks have become a tradition in high schools across the United States for graduating seniors. After all, graduation for Columbine seniors was less than four weeks away.

Although the popping noises were at first thought to be part of a senior day prank, Columbine students would soon realize that this was no playful prank committed by graduating seniors.

Soon after hearing the noise, Eric Harris and Dylan Klebold were observed entering the school's cafeteria wearing long black trench coats and brandishing an arsenal of weapons. The dark trench coats they wore were the symbol of what was known at the high school as the "Trench Coat Mafia." As shots rang out, students began to flee from the cafeteria. Teacher and coach Dave Sanders, who was attempting to help students out of the cafeteria, would become Harris and Klebold's first victim. Although Sanders's bravery undoubtedly helped save the lives of many students, tragically he was shot several times in the chest and shoulder as he attempted to protect students. Students realized that Sanders's wounds were extremely serious and attempted to stop the flow of blood from the mortally wounded teacher. Unfortunately, Sanders died from his wounds shortly after rescue teams arrived.

As a result of the gunfire, a number of 9-1-1 emergency calls were made to law enforcement to report the incidents occurring at Columbine High School. As law enforcement officials began responding to the school, Harris and Klebold calmly continued their rampage, going room by room, randomly shooting at students and teachers as they attempted to hide in bathrooms, underneath tables and chairs, and in storage areas. As police and rescue personnel arrived, they could hear gunfire and explosives coming from inside the school and observed students running from the building and jumping from the windows in an attempt to escape. Many of the students were crying and screaming, and many were injured and bleeding from gunshot wounds. As the students fled the building, police and rescue personnel attempted to assist them and tend to their injuries.

Once SWAT team members arrived at the scene, a plan was developed to locate the shooters. As police prepared to make their entry into the school, several bombs planted by Harris and Klebold were found in various locations around the building.

Obviously, law enforcement's primary goal was to evacuate the building as quickly as possible and to minimize injuries in case any of the bombs exploded. As SWAT officers cautiously entered the first floor of the building looking for additional victims and explosive devices, Harris and Klebold continued their assault on the second floor just above the police. The two killers went room by room looking for any students who were hiding in classrooms.

As Harris and Klebold entered the library, where moments earlier students were studying, several more students were shot. Students who survived the shooting in the library described how Harris and Klebold were laughing as they viciously shot their fellow students. From the library, Harris and Klebold then went to the science area classrooms. Several witnesses described how the two shooters would look through windows of the locked classrooms, actually making eye contact with a number of students, but did not shoot at any of these students. Other witnesses indicated that Harris and Klebold were shooting into empty classrooms and in one instance taped a

Molotov cocktail to the storage room door and then ignited it, causing a small fire in the storage room.

The suspects were then observed leaving the science area and entering the cafeteria, where a video camera recorded their actions at approximately 11:44 A.M. The videotape showed Harris squatting down and firing several shots at one of several propane bombs they had planted earlier in the cafeteria. It was later speculated that Harris was shooting at the propane bomb in an effort to get it to explode. Harris's efforts were unsuccessful. The videotape recording also showed Klebold examining the same bomb that Harris shot at and igniting what appeared to be a CO_2 cartridge, and throwing it at the propane bomb. Both shooters departed the cafeteria as the bomb was detonated. The cafeteria videotape showed that the detonation and subsequent fire occurred at about 11:46 A.M. The explosion caused the fire in the cafeteria, in turn setting off the fire alarm and sprinkler system. Fortunately, a large 20-pound propane bomb and a second bomb in a duffle bag nearby did not explode.

Harris and Klebold's random actions continued as they walked toward the school's main office area, where they fired shots into the office ceiling and in the art hallway to the north of the office. A school secretary and an unarmed security guard who had taken refuge in the office were able to make a 9-1-1 call to report Harris and Klebold's actions.

Continuing their random movements, Harris and Klebold returned to the cafeteria, where once again their images were captured on videotape. The images showed disappointment by Harris and Klebold, believed to have resulted from their maniacal plan not going as well as they intended. Most of the explosive devices they brought to the school did not detonate, and those devices that they were able to ignite were quickly put out by the sprinkler system. Damage from the explosive devices was minimal as compared to their intent of total destruction.

The cafeteria's video surveillance camera documented the duo leaving the cafeteria at 12 noon. Harris and Klebold returned once again to the library, where they shot through the library windows at police and rescue personnel who were on the outside of the school. Gunfire from the library was documented as occurring from about 12:02 P.M. to approximately 12:05 P.M. After that time period, no more shots could be confirmed as coming from Harris and Klebold. Although there were six survivors who were hiding in the library area, none was able to provide specific information as to when Harris and Klebold fired their last shots.

Even though shooting from inside the school ceased, law enforcement authorities still did not know for certain how many shooters were attacking Columbine High School, whether the shooters were dead, or whether they were hiding, waiting to surprise officers as they entered the school. SWAT members began a careful, methodical examination of each hallway and room in the school, looking for explosive devices, injured and dead students, and the perpetrators of this brutal attack on Columbine High School. Since authorities did not know the identity of the shooters or the number of shooters, each student who was rescued and evacuated had to be carefully searched for explosives and weapons. Finally, at about 4:00 P.M., law enforcement had completed its search of the building and announced that the building was secure. All survivors had been located and evacuated, and the bodies of the two killers were found in the library still clutching their weapons. Police announced that a total of 15 had died, including the shooters, Dylan Klebold and Eric Harris. According to the coroner's report, the deaths of both Harris and Klebold were consistent with self-inflicted gunshot wounds to the head. Investigators believed that Harris and Klebold killed themselves after returning to the library and shortly after shooting at law enforcement officers from the library windows.

Aftermath

Soon after the news spread of the first shooting at Columbine High School at about 11:35 A.M., the area's six hospitals were notified of the potential for mass casualties, and their emergency preparedness plans were put into effect. Twenty-five people were admitted into the hospitals, and of those 25, most had suffered gunshot wounds. Many of those admitted to area hospitals were in serious or critical condition.

Hundreds of frantic parents who had either heard news reports of the shootings or been contacted by family began arriving at Columbine High School. Parents waited and watched helplessly behind the police perimeter that had been established as students, teachers, and other employees ran from the school building to safety. Parents were frantically attempting to find their children, but because of the chaotic situation, it would be hours before they would learn whether their children were safe. Unfortunately, because of the complexity of the crime scene, the bodies of many of those killed at Columbine High School remained where they had fallen until after dark on April 21, more than 24 hours after the shooting began. Many families whose children had not been found waited helplessly for the identification of the dead to be released by authorities.

Investigation

Authorities from a number of jurisdictions in the Littleton area spent the next several months conducting one of the most exhaustive and intensive investigations in the state's history in an attempt to answer the question that preyed on everyone's mind: Why did this tragedy occur?

Eyewitnesses developed through the police investigations tentatively identified Eric Harris and Dylan Klebold as the two gunmen who attacked Columbine High School on April 20, 1999. Additional witnesses also believed that a third shooter was involved, but this report could never be confirmed. The identities of Harris and Klebold were positively made after their bodies were found in the library, where they died of self-inflicted gunshots to the head.

Early information developed by investigators from witness statements and crime scene findings was that Harris and Klebold were members of a group at Columbine High School known as the Trench Coat Mafia (TCM). Initially, 21 members of the TCM were identified through witness statements. These 21 individuals were interviewed by authorities, and from these individuals, an additional 20 associates of Harris and Klebold were identified and also interviewed. Although the investigation identified Harris and Klebold as "members" of the TCM, it was determined that the organization lacked structure and was not well organized like traditional street gangs. The origination of the TCM appeared to come from a group of students who wore black trench coats and were viewed by the student population as "misfits."

During the course of the investigation, it was determined through interviews that members of the TCM were often picked on and harassed by other students. In an attempt to determine the motive for the shootings and whether others had advance knowledge or took part in the planning of the attack on Columbine High School, nearly 100 individuals who had some connection to Harris and Klebold were interviewed. Additionally, more than 13 computers were seized and searched by authorities to determine whether others may have been involved in this horrific act, but no evidence was found to implicate any other individuals.

Several individuals interviewed by authorities were aware of Harris and Klebold's interest in pipe bombs, and a few actually had seen some of the bombs they had made. However, all those interviewed denied any knowledge that Harris and Klebold were planning to kill students at Columbine High School.

Evidence developed by investigators at the crime scene indicated that Harris and Klebold drove to the Columbine High School campus on April 20, 1999, armed with four guns, a number of knives, and a significant quantity of ammunition and explosive devices.

According to Jefferson County Sheriff's reports, Klebold was dressed in cargo pants, a black T-shirt, and a black trench coat. Underneath Klebold's coat was a 9-mm semiautomatic handgun attached to a strap slung over his shoulder. Additionally, Klebold was wearing cargo pants with large pockets that allowed him to conceal a 12-gauge shotgun with a sawed-off barrel.

Authorities also determined that Harris was wearing a black trench coat, enabling him to conceal a 9-mm carbine that was strapped to his shoulder. Harris also carried a 12-gauge pump shotgun in a duffel bag, with both the stock and the barrel cut down to make it more easily concealable.

The crime scene and forensic examination determined that Harris fired a total of 121 shots from a combination of the shotgun and 9-mm he carried. Klebold, it was determined, fired a total of 67 rounds from his shotgun and 9-mm weapon.

Investigators focused on how these two young killers could amass such a potent arsenal of weapons since Colorado law prohibited anyone from providing or permitting a juvenile under 18 years of age to possess a handgun. Through its extensive investigation, authorities learned that a female friend, Robyn Anderson, who was 18 years old, accompanied Harris and Klebold to a gun show in late 1998 and purchased shotguns and a rifle for the killers. These same weapons were used by Harris and Klebold to murder innocent students and faculty at Columbine. Robyn Anderson denied any knowledge of Harris and Klebold's plan. Since Colorado law does not pro- hibit the sale of a long gun (shotgun or rifle) from a private individual, Anderson could not be charged.

However, authorities charged Mark Manes, who they determined sold the 9-mm pistol to Dylan Klebold for $500. It was also determined that Manes purchased two boxes (100 rounds) of 9-mm ammunition for Eric Harris on April 19, the day before the attack on Columbine.

Manes entered a guilty plea to the charges of providing a handgun to a minor and possession of a dangerous weapon and was sentenced to six years in the Colorado Department of Correc- tions. Manes denied any knowledge of Harris and Klebold's plan.

During the course of the investigation, a third-shooter the- ory developed, as seven eyewitnesses remained firm in their account of seeing another shooter. These witnesses described the third person as wearing a white T-shirt and saw this indi- vidual throwing bombs and firing a gun. These statements conflicted with supporting evidence to include ballistics and other eyewitness testimony.

Through further investigation, authorities were able to explain the discrepancy in witness statements. Both Harris and Klebold were wearing black trench coats when they arrived at Columbine. After they began shooting, Harris took off his trench coat, exposing a white T-shirt. Harris's action of taking off the trench coat resulted in some witnesses believing that the person in the white T-shirt was the third shooter when it was actually Harris without his trench coat.

On the surface, before the Columbine attack, both Dylan Klebold and Eric Harris seemed like normal teenagers. Both boys were raised in upper-middle-class homes, and both were successful students. But investigators soon discovered that both Harris and Klebold were anything but normal. Both were fascinated with computers, and, as investigators learned, Har- ris had a website in which he expressed his anger toward the teachers and students at Columbine High School. Harris began posting material expressing his desire to seek revenge against anyone who annoyed him. He threatened to "blow up and shoot everything."

Harris and Klebold often bragged to other students that they would get revenge on the "jocks" at Columbine because they had treated them as outcasts. Harris and Klebold even made a video as a class project that showed them going through the school hallways carrying guns and shooting anyone in their path. Their teacher never permitted the video to be shown because of its violence. It was also widely known by other students that Harris and Klebold used the Internet to conduct research on how to make explosive devices.

Several teachers became increasingly concerned with Harris and Klebold's behavior and even reported their concerns to other school personnel; unfortunately, nothing was done because their actions did not result in any act for which they could be reported or punished. An exception to this was the previous year, when both boys had been suspended from school for hacking into the school's computer system. In spite of increasing concerns by teachers with Harris and Klebold's behavior and fascination with violence, parents of both boys maintained that they were never advised of their sons' behavior problems by school officials.

This lack of information exchange among authorities, school personnel, and parents enabled Harris and Klebold to continue down the path that resulted in them senselessly murdering 13 individuals at Columbine High School and then taking their own lives as well.

Conclusion

As with any violent crime event of this magnitude, a community is typically overcome with grief, sorrow, and shock at what transpired. The residents of Littleton spent the initial hours and days after the shootings mourning for those young lives that were senselessly taken. However, within several months of the incident, Littleton wanted answers and wanted someone held accountable for this tragic event.

At first, blame was directed at the Jefferson County Sheriff's office for not acting more quickly to save the lives of students and teachers who were victimized by Harris and Klebold. Police were accused of taking too long to enter the building, which many believed resulted in the death of teacher and coach Dave Sanders. Sanders lay wounded in the school for more than four hours after he was initially shot and before police evacuated him from the building.

Law enforcement defended its decision to delay its entry because of the number of undetonated bombs and the large number of rooms that had to be carefully searched.

Blame also focused on the parents of Dylan Klebold and Eric Harris. After all, weren't there signs they should have recognized that their sons' behavior was problematic? How could both boys have firearms and explosive materials in their homes without the parents being aware?

The Harris and Klebold families defended themselves, saying they were good parents and did not realize their sons were engaged in this type of antisocial behavior. Both sets of parents contended that at no time did the school notify them of any concern for the behavior of their sons, nor were they ever advised about the violent video their sons had made for a school project.

A number of lawsuits were filed by parents and family members of those killed and injured during the attack on Columbine High School. Those named in the suits included law enforcement officials, gun dealers, pharmaceutical companies (drugs prescribed to Harris), and the killers' parents.

Many of the lawsuits were settled or dismissed with confidentiality agreements. The largest settlement, involving a $1.5 million judgment against the Jefferson County Sheriff's office to the family of slain teacher Dave Sanders, was made public.

After a lengthy investigation, the Columbine Task Force, composed of a number of local, state, and federal law enforcement agencies, ultimately concluded that only Eric Harris and Dylan Klebold participated in the planning and carried out the shootings at Columbine High School on April 20, 1999. Additionally, they concluded that there was no evidence that anyone else assisted in the planning or had any prior knowledge of Harris and Klebold's plan.

However, the investigation revealed that there had been several incidents in the two years preceding the shooting that indicated Harris and Klebold's predisposition toward committing violent acts and that the police, school officials, and the shooters' parents were aware. This finding critically focused on the question as to whether this horrible and needless incident could have been prevented if appropriate intervention had occurred.

You're the Investigator

1. Discuss what you believe motivated Harris and Klebold to attack Columbine High School on April 20, 1999.

_____

_____

_____

_____

_____

_____

_____

_____

_____

_____

_____

2. Identify and discuss what prior behavior of Harris and Klebold was indicative of their violent tendencies.

_____

_____

_____

_____

_____

_____

_____

_____

_____

_____

_____

3. Describe how Harris and Klebold's involvement in the "Trench Coat Mafia" impacted the attack on Columbine High School.

_____

_____

_____

_____

_____

_____

_____

_____

_____

_____

4. On the basis of the available evidence, discuss why you believe or do not believe that Harris and Klebold, alone, carried out the shootings at Columbine High School.

_____

_____

_____

_____

_____

_____

_____

_____

_____

_____

5. Discuss whether you believe that certain types of information, like bomb-making information, should be available via the computer for anyone to access.

_____

_____

_____

_____

_____

_____

_____

_____

_____

_____

_____

6. Describe what you believe to be the legal theory and basis for the family of coach and teacher, Dave Sanders, to successfully sue the Jefferson County Sheriff's office.

_____

_____

_____

_____

_____

_____

_____

_____

_____

_____

_____

7. Why do you think school violence is on the rise across the
   United States, and what can we do to prevent it?

_____

_____

_____

_____

_____

_____

_____

_____

_____

_____

_____

8. What actions could Columbine school authorities have taken
   to prevent Harris and Klebold's shooting spree at the school?

_____

_____

_____

_____

_____

_____

_____

_____

_____

_____

_____

9. Discuss the role of violence in the media and what impact it has on juvenile crime.

_____

_____

_____

_____

_____

_____

_____

_____

_____

_____

_____

10. Discuss whether you believe that stricter gun-control laws would reduce violent crime committed by juveniles, such as the massacre at Columbine High School.

_____

_____

_____

_____

_____

_____

_____

_____

_____

_____

_____

CHAPTER 3

Murder or Wrestling? The Lionel Tate Story

The story of Lionel Tate is an all-too-familiar story of a child who bounced back and forth between two divorced parents, one living in Mississippi and the other in Florida. The parents alternated custody of Lionel, resulting in the boy attending a number of different schools during his childhood.

Because of his personality and temperament, Tate had difficulty making friends, and as a result, he became a lonely child who often exhibited behavioral problems to get the attention he craved.

According to his fourth-grade teacher in Mississippi, Mrs. Stockstill, Lionel Tate was a loner who was very loud and boisterous and a child who was often "out of control." According to Tate's fifth-grade teacher at Watkins Elementary School in Hollywood, Florida, none of the students in her class wanted to sit next to Tate, and most of her students did not get along with Tate. Tate was accused of stealing other students' books, pencils, and any other property of students he wanted.

Because of his continuing behavioral problems, another teacher, Ms. Lopez, recommended that Tate be sent to another school that specialized in students with behavioral problems; unfortunately, that school had no vacancies.

When Tate's mother, Kathleen Grossett-Tate, went to the Florida Highway Patrol Academy to become a trooper, Lionel was once again sent back to Mississippi to live with his father. While in school in Mississippi, Lionel continued his disruptive demeanor and was written up numerous times for behavior problems. Lionel also began exhibiting behavior problems at home; in fact, after one incident, Lionel's stepmother called one of his teachers and complained about his behavior and asked for recommendations on how to handle Tate. When the school year ended, Tate returned to Florida to live with his mother.

On his return to Florida, Tate's behavior problems in school continued, eventually resulting in his reading teacher, Ms. Foley, contacting Tate's mother to discuss his problematic demeanor. When Kathleen Grossett-Tate arrived at the school, she was wearing her state trooper uniform. However, during the discussion about Lionel, Kathleen Grossett-Tate seemed content to blame others for Lionel's behavior problems.

Lionel Tate was once again sent back to Mississippi to live with his father. Lionel's behavior problems worsened, and he became more impulsive. For his age, Lionel was much bigger than other children his age, and as a consequence, he had a tendency to bully other students and playmates. It was also noted that Lionel was increasingly becoming more hostile toward authority and vulgar in his communication.

Although Lionel's schoolwork was generally good, even occasionally getting Bs, his behavior resulted in numerous suspensions, which totaled 18 days during that school year.

At the conclusion of the school year, Lionel Tate was once again sent back to Florida to live with his mother.

Investigation

On July 28, 1999, Lionel Tate's mother, Kathleen Grossett-Tate, agreed to watch a friend's six-year-old daughter, Tiffany Eunick. Tate's mother and Tiffany's mother grew up together in Jamaica and had known each other before moving to the United States. Although Lionel and Tiffany had known each other for only a few weeks, the children had played together previously without incident when Tate's mother had been asked to watch Tiffany.

After fixing the children dinner, Lionel's mother allowed the children to watch television and then went upstairs to her bedroom. At approximately 10:00 P.M., Kathleen Grossett-Tate would later tell investigators that the children's play became loud and that she hollered for them to quiet down. About 40 minutes later, Lionel Tate came up to his mother's room and told her that Tiffany wasn't breathing.

Lionel Tate initially claimed that he and Tiffany were playing and that he put Tiffany in a headlock and banged her head on a table. At the time of this incident, Tiffany Eunick was six years old and weighed 48 pounds, while Lionel Tate was 12 years old and weighed nearly 170 pounds.

Initially, police investigators could not detect any other injuries. However, a subsequent medical examiner's investigation and report indicated that Eunick suffered more than 35 injuries. A number of these injuries were extremely serious, including a fractured skull, brain contusions, a ruptured spleen, a partially detached liver, numerous bruises and lacerations, and a damaged rib cage.

After examining the evidence generated from the police investigation, medical examiner's report, and analysis by child abuse experts, the Broward County State Attorney's office presented the case to the Broward County Grand Jury, and Lionel Tate was subsequently indicted on felony murder charges as an adult.

Trial

During Tate's trial, the prosecution presented evidence that although Tate's actions were not premeditated, Tate did commit felony murder by seriously beating Tiffany Eunick to the point that her cumulative injuries resulted in her death. Expert witnesses for the prosecution provided testimony that because of the number and nature of Tiffany Eunick's injuries, the duration of the beating would have occurred over a period of between one to five minutes. The prosecutor also demonstrated that after the beating, Tate admitted watching Tiffany urinate in her pants and roll around on the floor in pain while he went back to watching television. Tate would later go get his mother when he determined that Tiffany was not breathing.

Tate ultimately admitted that he jumped from the stair-case with his nearly 170-pound body, landing on the 48-pound six-year-old's body. Tate also admitted to punching Eunick with his fist between 35 and 40 times.

Prosecutors also presented testimony that Tiffany Eunick's injuries were the equivalent of being thrown from a second- or third-story building. Prosecutors argued that Lionel Tate was 12 years old at the time of the incident and that he had a normal IQ. Tate was not slow, mentally retarded, or mentally ill but rather a street-smart kid who had a history of significant behavioral problems that included fighting, stealing, and more than 15 school suspensions.

Ken Padowitz, the Broward County assistant state attorney who handled the Tate prosecution, was quoted as saying, "This was not child's play or roughhousing. Tiffany and the defendant were not playmates, having known each other only two to four weeks and being separated by six grade levels. Not in the wildest imagination would a playground fight or household roughhousing, which results in accidental injury or death, compare to this prolonged and brutal homicidal beating."

During the presentation of Lionel Tate's defense, his attorney argued that Tate did not understand the difference between simulated violence, which he learned from watching professional wrestling on television, and the repercussions of real violence. The defense attempted to argue that professional wrestling was responsible for Tate's actions the night he killed Tiffany Eunick. Tate's attorney argued that professional wrestlers in their bizarre outfits promoted violence and had no regard for the negative impact and influence their antics had on children.

Tate's attorney even attempted to subpoena professional wrestlers Hulk Hogan and The Rock, but the trial judge refused to let them testify. Tate's attorney wanted the wrestlers to demonstrate how they make their actions appear authentic.

After nearly a two-week trial, the jury found Lionel Tate, at the time 14 years old, guilty of first-degree murder. Based on comments from several jurors, the jury seemed more focused on the gruesome violence than the influence that television and professional wrestling had on Lionel Tate.

Juror William Stevenson later said, "The injuries were so extensive we all felt that wasn't an accident. We had to abide by the law, and the law spelled it out. It wasn't just wrestling."

Another juror, Elise Schifano, told the local newspaper, "Our biggest problem was convicting a child of an adult crime." Ms. Schifano also stated, "We had no idea what sentence he would face."

The trial judge also did not accept the defense argument that Tate thought it was okay to body-slam Tiffany Eunick and that she would walk away unhurt. The judge was also quoted as saying, "It is inconceivable that such injuries could be caused by roughhousing or horseplay or by replicating wrestling moves."

Following the guidelines of state law, which require that an individual convicted of first-degree murder must serve life in prison without parole, the judge imposed the sentence on Lionel Tate. In imposing the sentence, the judge described Tate's killing of Tiffany Eunick as "cold, callous, and indescribably cruel."

In 2001, almost two years after Tiffany Eunick's death, Lionel Tate would become the youngest individual in the United States to be sentenced to life in prison without the possibility of parole.

Tate served three years in a juvenile detention facility until his conviction was overturned in 2003 by an appeals court because he was not afforded a competency hearing prior to his trial. As a part of a plea deal with the state, Tate would not be retried if he agreed to plead guilty to second-degree murder. As part of the agreement, Tate was given credit for time served and was released from prison on January 26, 2004, Tate's seventeenth birthday. The terms of Tate's release from prison also included ten years of probation and a year of house arrest, and he was mandated to wear a monitoring device.

Tate's Troubles Continue

Lionel Tate returned to his home near Pembroke Park, Florida, to live with his mother. By September 2004, Tate was once again in trouble with the law. He was arrested by police officers near his home at 2:00 A.M. for possession of a knife. The trial judge extended Tate's probation to 15 years and sternly warned the teen that if he violated the terms of his probation again, he would put him behind bars.

Undaunted by the judge's warning, by the following May, Tate was once again in serious trouble. On May 23, 2005, Lionel Tate was charged with armed robbery, armed burglary, battery, and violation of probation when he confronted a pizza delivery man with a handgun outside a friend's apartment after ordering the pizza. After being confronted by Tate, who was holding a handgun, the pizza delivery man dropped the pizzas and ran from the scene. Tate allegedly then went back into the apartment, where he assaulted one of the residents who did not want him in the apartment. In the meantime, the pizza delivery man made a 9-1-1 call to police to report the robbery.

Police officers responding to the scene arrested Tate, who was subsequently identified by the pizza delivery man as the person who robbed him. Officers did not recover the gun used by Tate.

Conclusion

On March 1, 2006, Tate pled guilty to the armed robbery charge, and Judge Lazarus scheduled sentencing for April 3, 2006. Judge Lazarus ordered Tate held without bail until his sentencing. In addition to the armed robbery charge, Tate also faced weapons charges and probation violation. It appeared that Judge Lazarus would have the probation violation sentence run concurrently with the armed robbery sentence.

In a series of legal maneuvers, Tate's attorney subsequently had Tate withdraw his guilty plea to armed robbery, instead having Tate plead guilty to the weapon's possession charge.

On May 18, 2006, Lionel Tate, now 19 years of age, was sentenced to 30 years in prison by Judge Lazarus on gun-possession charges and probation violation, bringing to a conclusion a very sad set of circumstances that led to the death of six-year-old Tiffany Eunick and now the imprisonment of Tate for 30 years.

As a final chapter in the tragic story, Tate's mother, a Florida Highway Patrol trooper, reported her service weapon missing, which was subsequently found in the possession of Tate and a friend. The Florida Highway Patrol conducted an internal investigation in which they found Trooper Grossett-Tate negligent in the handling of her Florida Highway Patrol–issued weapon. Trooper Grossett-Tate was subsequently reprimanded by the Florida Highway Patrol for her failure to properly secure her weapon.

You're the Investigator

1. Describe the indicators in Lionel Tate's life and behavior patterns that would be predictors of Tate's later legal problems.

   _____

   _____

   _____

   _____

   _____

   _____

   _____

   _____

   _____

   _____

   _____

2. Describe the factors in Tate's family life and relationships that may have caused him to develop antisocial behavioral attitudes.

   _____

   _____

   _____

   _____

   _____

_____

_____

_____

_____

_____

_____

3. Discuss whether you believe that Lionel Tate's mother's actions or inactions contributed to Lionel's behavioral and legal problems.

_____

_____

_____

_____

_____

_____

_____

_____

_____

_____

4. Discuss the importance of the medical examiner's investigation and report in the prosecution of Lionel Tate.

_____

_____

_____

_____

_____

_____

---

5. Discuss the difference between premeditated murder and felony murder.

---

6. Discuss the prosecution's theory regarding Tate's culpability for Tiffany Eunick's death.

_____

_____

_____

7. Describe why you believe that the defense's argument did not convince jurors of Lionel Tate's innocence.

_____

_____

_____

_____

_____

_____

_____

_____

_____

_____

_____

8. Discuss your philosophy as to whether juvenile criminals should be punished as adults and whether Lionel Tate's initial sentence was appropriate.

_____

_____

_____

_____

_____

_____

_____

_____

_____

_____

9. Describe why you believe it was appropriate (or not) for Judge Lazarus to withhold bail for Tate after he pled guilty but prior to his sentencing on armed robbery charges.

_____

_____

_____

_____

_____

_____

_____

_____

_____

_____

_____

10. Do you believe that watching wrestling on T.V. contributed to Tate's actions?

_____

_____

_____

_____

_____

_____

_____

_____

_____

_____

_____

CHAPTER 4

The Allentown Stalker

A series of gruesome assaults and murders began in mid-1992 in Allentown, Pennsylvania, that would terrorize the community and result in an extensive investigation by police and the district attorney's office to capture a violent young serial killer.

The Victims

The killer's first attack occurred on August 9, 1992, at the apartment of 29-year-old Joan May Burghardt. Burghardt was unaware that a man was watching her through her apartment window as she undressed. After changing clothes, Burghardt walked into her living room carrying a glass of milk and some cookies. No sooner had Burghardt entered the living room than the man tore the front window screen and climbed into Burghardt's apartment. Before Burghardt had a chance to react, the intruder hit her in the head, knocking her glasses off and causing her blood to splatter onto a nearby wall. Although dazed from the blow to her head, Burghardt was able to run past the intruder to another room where she began screaming for help. Later, a neighbor, living above Burghardt's apartment, told police he heard the screams but decided not to get involved.

As Burghardt continued to scream, the intruder turned up the volume on the television to cover her screams. The intruder then began beating Burghardt with a blunt object until she fell to the floor unconscious. In all, Burghardt suffered more than 30 blows to the head and face. Once the killer realized that Burghardt was dead, he took a pair of the victim's underwear and used them to masturbate over her dead body. Authorities later learned that after completing the assault, the killer, whose clothes where covered in blood, left through a back door and walked to his home a few blocks away.

Although authorities were unaware at the time, the killer was arrested a short time later for another crime and spent eight months in juvenile detention. On his release, the killer began stalking his second victim, Charlotte Schmoyer.

During the morning of June 9, 1993, a resident on East Gordon Street in Allentown was looking out her window for her morning newspaper, which was late, when she noticed the newspaper girl's bicycle abandoned between two parked vehicles. Being concerned for the girl's safety, the resident called police.

Police responded to the area and began searching for the newspaper girl, Charlotte Schmoyer. Police contacted her supervisor at the paper and her parents, neither of whom had heard from Charlotte. As officers began searching the area, they found a portable radio belonging to the 15-year-old. With their fears and concerns of foul play increasing, authorities expanded their search and after several hours discovered a trail of blood leading into a reservoir area. Authorities soon discovered a discarded shoe, and then their worst fears were confirmed when a searcher discovered the body of Charlotte Schmoyer, which had been covered with leaves and tree branches. Although authorities had no witnesses to the crime itself, several residents reported seeing a blue car in the vicinity of Schmoyer's bicycle and also near the reservoir.

Authorities conducted an autopsy that confirmed that Schmoyer had been raped and stabbed more than 20 times in the upper torso and that her throat had been slashed with a knife. During the forensic inspection of Schmoyer's body, a pubic hair not belonging to the girl was found on her clothing, and a head hair was found on her knee. These items of hair were maintained by authorities to compare with any suspects who might later be developed.

Police determined that the perpetrator spotted Charlotte in the early morning hours as she was tending to her paper route and that as the young girl rode her bike toward his car, the killer grabbed her and forced Charlotte into his vehicle. Police believe the killer then drove to the reservoir area, where he brutally raped and stabbed the girl.

Charlotte Schmoyer was the second female to be killed in this area in less than a year. Both law enforcement officials and the community were shocked at the brutality of both murders and began to wonder whether these were random attacks or whether a serial killer was on the loose in this normally quiet community. Authorities had no suspects in either Burghardt's or Schmoyer's murder.

Denise and John Cali lived in a neighborhood of Allentown near where Charlotte Schmoyer had been abducted. Denise would regularly walk about a mile from her home to the business she and her husband operated. Denise only later learned that when she made the trip from her home to their business, she was being stalked by the Allentown killer.

During the early summer of 1993, the Calis went out of town for a few days, only to return to discover that their house had been burglarized. As John Cali looked through the house to determine what was missing, he discovered that a bag containing his gun collection was gone from a closet where he kept it. The Calis called the police to report the burglary. With all his weapons taken and concerned that the burglar might return, John Cali immediately purchased two new guns that he wanted his wife to learn to shoot.

In the meantime, just several days after the Cali burglary, the same intruder entered the home of another woman he had been stalking in the same neighborhood. When the intruder discovered that the woman was in an upstairs bedroom with her boyfriend, he backed away not wanting to confront the male. The intruder, still determined to have a victim, discovered the woman's five-year-old daughter in another bedroom in the house.

The intruder immediately choked the girl until she passed out. He carried her downstairs and raped her. As she started to regain consciousness, he once again choked her until she passed out. The intruder then left the house and went to his home, which was only blocks away.

As the girl regained consciousness, she went to her mother's bedroom to report what happened. The mother's boyfriend searched the house and found a screen missing from a window. The mother took the child to the doctor, who examined the child and verified she had been choked and sexually assaulted.

As word of the attack on the child spread, the residents of Allentown became more frightened. Residents who normally left their windows open during the summer heat were now taking security precautions. On June 28, 1993, the "Allentown Stalker" decided to revisit Denise and John Cali's home, as he had watched Denise walking in the neighborhood and had previously burglarized the house when the Calis were not at home.

On the evening of June 28, Denise Cali was home alone because her husband was out of town on a business trip. Denise expected him back sometime during the night, but no definite time for his return was known. Denise had just returned home from a relative's house who lived down the street. Denise was nervous being in the house alone because of the recent attacks on two women in their neighborhood and because of their own previous burglary, when her husband's guns were stolen.

On returning to her house, Denise Cali changed clothes and got ready for bed. Before crawling into bed, she opened a bedroom window because the house was quite warm. Cali was very uncomfortable about being home alone and could not fall asleep. Cali laid quietly in bed listening to the nighttime sounds that filled the air. Suddenly, Cali heard a noise coming from inside the house, and she realized she was not alone. Cali screamed out hoping to frighten the intruder into leaving but did not hear any indication that the intruder was gone. Frightened and not sure what to do, Cali decided to go to the neighbor's house. As she ran from her bedroom down a hallway, she was confronted by a man armed with a knife who stepped from a closet where he was hiding.

As Cali attempted to exit the house through a door, the intruder grabbed her by the arm and stabbed her in the lip. As Cali struggled with her attacker, she was able to knock the knife from his hand and punch her way past him as she ran outside. Her attacker followed her outside and knocked her to the ground, striking her in the face multiple times. As she tried to scream, the attacker held her down and began choking her until she was unconscious. During the struggle, Cali was able to bite her attacker before losing consciousness.

A neighbor heard the noise of a struggle and turned on floodlights, which frightened the attacker, who ran from the scene. After regaining consciousness, Cali was able to get back to her house and make a 9-1-1 call to police. Cali was transported to a local hospital for treatment of her injuries, which consisted of bruises, strangulation marks on her neck, and a severe cut to her lip. While at the hospital, Cali was also administered a rape test kit to determine whether she had been sexually assaulted while she was unconscious. The investigation confirmed that Cali had been sexually assaulted.

John Cali was stunned when he was advised about the attack on his wife. John immediately made plans to tighten security at their home. When Denise Cali's condition permitted, she gave authorities a detailed description of her assailant. Ms. Cali described her attacker as a young white male, about 5 feet, 7 inches, with a muscular build and no beard.

Area newspapers ran stories concerning the Cali attack, and now both authorities and the Calis were concerned that she would be targeted again by the killer since she was the only victim who could identify him.

The Calis took additional security measures at their home to include installing a burglar alarm. In spite of the alarm, the intruder was able to break in again while the Calis were gone and steal a new .38-caliber automatic pistol that was purchased after Mr. Cali's gun collection was stolen.

Authorities believed that the killer would likely attempt to murder Denise Cali so that she could never testify against him. Police and the district attorney's office developed a plan with the Calis' consent for the Calis to remain in their home and to place a police officer in the home to catch the killer when he attempted to return to the Cali house. Without anyone's knowledge, a police officer was assigned to the Cali residence to trap the killer if he returned.

While the authorities were executing their plan to catch the killer at the Cali residence, the serial killer/rapist located another victim in a nearby neighborhood. The killer had stalked Jessica Fortney, a 47-year-old woman who lived with her daughter, son-in-law, and their seven-year-old daughter.

On July 14, 1993, the assailant broke into the residence, and while the daughter, son-in-law, and granddaughter slept upstairs, the killer attacked Fortney downstairs, breaking her nose and then raping and strangling her to death. The killer left Fortney's blood-soaked body on a sofa in the living room.

Although the killer was unaware, Fortney's granddaughter observed the attack from her room. The description provided by the girl corresponded with the description Denise Cali gave of her attacker. Authorities were now convinced that a dangerous serial killer/rapist had attacked all the women in the area. Authorities now worried when and where the killer would attack next. On the basis of the pattern and time frames of the previous attacks, it was believed that another attack would happen within days.

Officers concealed inside the Cali residence remained especially vigilant, even though two weeks had passed since the murder of Jessica Fortney. Then, suddenly, at about 9:30 P.M., the officer assigned to the Cali residence heard a noise coming from the patio area and then heard someone attempting to open the front door, which did not open. The officer then observed a hand reach through the living room window and remove the screen. The officer then pressed a silent alarm on his police radio to have help dispatched to his location. Backup was now en route to the Cali residence.

Suddenly, the officer observed the living room window open, and a short, husky, young man climbed into the room. The officer shouted at the intruder to halt and announced, "Police." The intruder ran past the officer toward the kitchen and pulled a gun from his pants. The officer pulled his gun and fired at the intruder several times. The man kept running and fired back at the officer. Both the officer and the intruder exchanged several more shots in the kitchen area. The officer went to the Cali's bedroom to tell them to stay down as he prepared to confront the suspect again. As the officer carefully moved toward the kitchen, he noticed several broken windows through which the intruder had escaped despite the fact that responding officers were covering the perimeter of the house. On further examination of the door through which the intruder escaped, authorities observed a large amount of blood. It was unknown whether the killer was wounded in the shoot-out or whether he received a bad cut from the glass.

Police immediately notified area hospitals to be on the lookout for anyone who matched the suspect's description who was seeking treatment for either a bullet wound or other significant injuries. At about 5:30 A.M., a young man appeared at an area hospital seeking treatment for severe cuts to his leg and arm. As the suspect realized that authorities were waiting for him, he attempted to flee from the hospital but was caught as he attempted to exit.

The officer who exchanged shots with the intruder went to the hospital and positively identified him as the man who broke into the Cali residence and shot at the officer. The suspect was identified as Harvey "Miggy" Robinson, who recently turned 18, making him a juvenile when his reign of terror on Allentown began nearly a year earlier. The Calis were immediately notified of Robinson's capture, and at least now they could rest knowing that Denise Cali's attacker could no longer target her.

Investigation and Evidence

After Robinson's arrest, he was charged with numerous felonies in connection with the attacks on Denise Cali. Charges included attempted murder, burglary, and aggravated assault. Bond for Robinson was set at $1 million.

Authorities immediately began an intensive investigation to secure evidence that could be utilized in Robinson's trial. Denise Cali was able to positively identify Robinson as the man who attacked her. Robinson also had a bite mark that Denise Cali stated she inflicted on her attacker. Police were able to recover a .38-caliber gun from Robinson's bedroom that was previously stolen from the Cali residence. Forensic and ballistic examinations of casings recovered inside the Cali residence that were fired by the intruder on July 31, 1993, also matched the .38-caliber weapon recovered at Robinson's home.

In addition, police obtained search warrants and searched a light blue Ford belonging to Robinson's mother that matched the basic description of a suspect vehicle observed in the neighborhood where Charlotte Schmoyer was abducted and killed. Authorities also searched Robinson's gray Dodge. Blood from

Robinson was discovered in both vehicles, pointing to the fact that he drove both cars on the night he was injured, during the shootout with police, and while breaking into the Cali residence.

Several months later, authorities got an additional break when DNA tests from Robinson's blood matched DNA from semen in the three murder/rape cases (Burghardt, Schmoyer, and Fortney) and the rapes of Denise Cali and the five-year-old girl. Additional DNA evidence linked hair and blood found on Schmoyer to Robinson.

The first of the cases to be scheduled for trial by the district attorney's office was the Denise Cali case. As a result of overwhelming evidence gathered by authorities, Robinson agreed to plead guilty to the charges of rape, assault, and burglary involving Ms. Cali as well as shooting at the police officer who was hiding in the Cali residence. At the sentencing, Robinson's defense attorney argued for leniency; however, the district attorney cited Robinson's lengthy juvenile record, antisocial behavior, and viciousness of the attacks in his argument to the court. The judge sentenced Robinson to between 40 and 80 years in prison for his crimes against Denise Cali and the police officer.

Now that the district attorney had successfully prosecuted Robinson on the Cali case, the death penalty cases would be the next legal battle facing Robinson. Robinson's defense attorney filed motions with the court to have three separate trials on the murder cases (Burghardt, Schmoyer, and Fortney). The district attorney, on the other hand, argued for one trial involving all three victims. The court agreed with the state's argument.

When the trial began, the district attorney presented more than 40 witnesses along with compelling and convincing forensic and DNA evidence that linked Robinson to all three murders/rapes. After a three-week trial, Harvey Miguel Robinson was found guilty of the murders/rapes of all three women.

Conclusion

During the sentencing hearing, with Robinson's life in jeopardy, the district attorney argued that the Robinson case was a classic death penalty case in that Robinson's crimes involved multiple murder victims, torture of the victims, and murders committed during other felony crimes and that Robinson had a long history of violent, aggressive, antisocial behavior. To emphasize his point with jurors, the district attorney displayed the gruesome photographs of the victims to show jurors the violent nature of Robinson's attacks.

On November 10, 1994, the jury recommended to the court that Robinson be sentenced to death by lethal injection. Robinson was placed on Pennsylvania's death row pending his execution. Over a period of nearly ten years on death row, Robinson filed numerous appeals in an attempt to save his own life. In December 2005, the Pennsylvania Supreme Court affirmed the first-degree murder convictions in the Burghardt and Schmoyer cases but vacated the death sentence in those two cases. However, the court did affirm the death sentence in the Fortney case. In addition, on March 1, the U.S. Supreme Court issued a ruling that juveniles under the age of 17 were not eligible for the death penalty. Although the U.S. Supreme Court decision overruled Robinson's death sentence in the Burghardt murder, which was committed when he was 17 years old, his death sentence in the Fortney murder remained, as he was an adult when that crime was committed.

Robinson appealed his death penalty sentence in the Fortney case to the U.S. Supreme Court, and in October of 2005, the Court rejected his request. The Supreme Court decision cleared the way for Pennsylvania Governor Ed Rendell to sign Robinson's death warrant with an execution date of April 2006. Further appeals have delayed the execution, but Robinson to date remains on Pennsylvania's death row pending his execution.

You're the Investigator

1. Describe and discuss the evidence that the juvenile killer left at the scene of Joan Burghardt's murder.

_____

_____

_____

_____

_____

_____

_____

_____

_____

_____

_____

_____

2. Describe how Robinson chose his victims.

_____

_____

_____

_____

_____

_____

_____

_____

_____

_____

_____

3. Describe and discuss what information led authorities to discover the body of Robinson's second victim, Charlotte Schmoyer.

_____

_____

_____

_____

_____

_____

_____

_____

_____

_____

_____

_____

4. Discuss the evidence authorities recovered at the scene of
   the Schmoyer murder/rape that later would help identify
   her killer.

_____

_____

_____

_____

_____

_____

_____

_____

_____

_____

_____

5. Describe the elements that existed that caused authorities
   to declare that Allentown was being preyed on by a serial
   murderer/rapist.

_____

_____

_____

_____

_____

_____

_____

_____

_____

_____

_____

6. Discuss the physical and forensic evidence that linked Robinson to the Denise Cali assault.

_____

_____

_____

_____

_____

_____

_____

_____

_____

_____

_____

7. Describe the investigation plan authorities used to capture Denise Cali's attacker.

_____

_____

_____

_____

_____

_____

_____

_____

_____

_____

_____

_____

8. Discuss the evidence that linked Robinson to the shoot-out with authorities at the Cali residence and how authorities acquired the evidence.

_____

_____

_____

_____

_____

_____

_____

_____

_____

_____

9. Discuss what issues the prosecutor believed jurors should have taken into consideration as they deliberated on Robinson's sentencing.

_____

_____

_____

_____

_____

_____

_____

_____

_____

_____

_____

10. How did a U.S. Supreme Court decision on juvenile mur-
    der defendants affect Robinson's case? Why you believe
    the Supreme Court issued that decision?

_____

_____

_____

_____

_____

_____

_____

_____

_____

_____

_____

_____

CHAPTER 5

Lesbian Killers

Carl and Sarah Collier, who wanted to have children of their own but could not, decided to adopt a son and daughter. Their adopted son, Devin, successfully followed in his adopted father's footsteps in being active in his church and working for Delta Airlines. The Colliers were very proud of their son and enjoyed a close relationship. Their adopted daughter, Carla Harvey, however, took a different direction. Carla had two daughters by two different men. Carla was frequently in trouble with authorities and was ultimately arrested and convicted on drug charges. She was sentenced to prison in the spring of 2004.

At the time of Carla's imprisonment, the Colliers, in their seventies and retired, decided to have Carla's 15-year-old daughter, Holly Harvey, live with them. Holly's father was unable to adequately care for his daughter as a result of being confined to a wheelchair because of a severe car accident. The Colliers quickly learned that young Holly was a difficult child to control, refused to follow rules, and continually ran away from home. Regardless of how much empathy and love the Colliers showed to their granddaughter, it was never reciprocated. In fact, Holly's behavior only worsened. Holly was having trouble at school and began using drugs. During this time, Holly developed a close friendship with 16-year-old Sandra Ketchum and engaged in a lesbian relationship with her friend.

Holly's animosity toward her grandparents worsened by the day as they imposed more rules on the teenager, trying to change the direction of her life. The grandparents attempted to get Holly involved in church activities, but she refused to cooperate. In one final attempt to get Holly to change, the Colliers told her she could no longer see her lover, Sandra Ketchum.

Authorities later discovered a poem written by Holly in which she wrote about how depressed and miserable she was and that she frequently cried herself to sleep because her grandparents forbade her to use drugs and refused to let her see Sandy Ketchum. In the poem, Holly wrote, "All I want to do is kill."

Holly's lover, Sandy Ketchum, also had a difficult childhood. According to various reports, Ketchum's mother abandoned her when she was only 15 months old, leaving the girl to be raised by three different stepmothers, one of whom was reportedly physically abusive toward the girl. Because of these experiences, Sandy searched for a loving relationship with a female whom she could trust. The love between Sandy and Holly created a strong bond between the teenagers that would cause them to do anything to protect each other.

A Plan to Kill

As Holly's relationship with Sandy grew stronger, her resentment toward her grandparents, who wanted to keep her away from Sandy, worsened. The two lovers developed a plan to kill Holly's grandparents so that the two girls could live their lives as they wanted, without interference or control from the Colliers.

Neither Holly nor Sandy was clandestine about the plot; they would openly talk with friends about acquiring a gun and killing Holly's grandparents. Although the girls were unable to obtain a gun, they were able to find several dangerous knives to carry out their plan.

In spite of her grandparent's directive, on Wednesday, August 2, 2004, Holly was able to let Sandy into her basement bedroom. The girls developed a detailed plan on how they would carry out the murders of Holly's grandparents. Authorities discovered later that Holly wrote a "to-do" list on her arm in ink. The list read "kill, keys, money, and jewelry."

While working on their plan to kill the Colliers, the girls began smoking marijuana laced with cocaine. The grandparents, who were upstairs, smelled the odor of the marijuana coming from the basement and decided to investigate. As the grandparents were coming down the steps, the girls heard them, and Sandy Ketchum, who was armed with a knife, quickly hid behind the bed. When the grandparents confronted Holly about the drug odor, Holly pulled out a knife and immediately began stabbing her grandmother multiple times in the upper torso. Holly screamed out for help from her girlfriend. Sandy Ketchum jumped from her hiding location and helped Holly stab her grandmother to death. During the attack, Sarah Collier received more than 20 stab wounds to her upper torso and back.

Although suffering from stab wounds himself, Carl Collier was able to break free from the duo and run upstairs in an attempt to get to a phone to call police. Holly chased her grandfather upstairs and cut the phone line as he attempted to call police. Holly then repeatedly stabbed her grandfather until he collapsed on the kitchen floor mortally wounded. Carl Collier was left face down on the floor, lying in a pool of blood, with more than 15 stab wounds to his neck and chest.

After killing Carl and Sarah Collier, the teenagers executed the remainder of their vicious plan. With both girls soaked in Holly's grandparents' blood, they searched the house and located the keys to the Colliers' pickup truck. Both girls continued to rummage through the house searching for cash and jewelry. The duo found jewelry that they placed in a bag with clean clothes and then fled from the house in Holly's grandfather's truck.

The girls, who were still in blood-soaked clothing, drove to Griffin, Georgia, to Holly's friend Sara's house. When Sara inquired as to why they were soaked in blood, the girls initially said they were victims of a mugging and had been injured in the attack. After showering and changing clothes, Holly told Sara the truth about why they had blood on them. After hearing what had really happened, Sara told the girls they had to leave her house. After Holly and Sandy left Sara's house, Sara told her parents about the gruesome murders and also contacted police.

The Investigation

The Fayette County Sheriff's office began an immediate investigation. Officers were sent to the Collier residence, where they discovered the gruesome crime scene and the bodies of Carl and Sarah Collier. Authorities immediately broadcasted a description of the stolen truck based on information at the scene and information provided by Sara that Holly admitted to killing her grandparents. On the basis of this information, authorities were able to obtain arrest warrants for both Holly Harvey and Sandy Ketchum.

After leaving Sara's house, the girls headed for a beach area on Tybee Island, just outside Savannah, Georgia. Although the girls were unaware, authorities began tracking their every move through cell phone calls to friends as they drove throughout the evening.

While at the beach, Holly and Sandy met two brothers whose parents had just moved into a new house in the area. The girls told the boys they had nowhere to stay and wanted to pawn jewelry that was left to them by their grandmother. Although the boys refused to help the girls pawn the jewelry, the boys' parents gave permission for the girls to spend the night. Early the next morning, to the surprise of the family, the household was awakened by more than 20 police officers who had surrounded the house. Police were able to pinpoint Holly and Sandy's location through their cell phone transmissions and the Colliers' stolen pickup truck.

Holly Harvey and Sandy Ketchum were arrested without incident, but according to Lieutenant Colonel Bruce Jordan of the Fayette County Sheriff's office, Holly Harvey was "callous and cocky" and demonstrated no remorse for the terrible crimes committed against her grandparents. Sandy Ketchum, on the other hand, was remorseful and agreed to cooperate with authorities.

After the girls' arrest, investigators searched the stolen truck and found a bag that contained bloody clothes and two bloody knives. Harvey and Ketchum were charged as adults with armed robbery and two counts of felony murder for the deaths of Carl and Sarah Collier. In the decision to charge the girls as adults, authorities cited the brutality of the crimes, premeditation, and that both defendants recognized the consequences of their actions.

On April 14, 2005, Holly Harvey pled guilty to two counts of murder and was sentenced to two consecutive life sentences. She will be eligible for parole in 20 years. Sandy Ketchum was sentenced to three life terms for murder and armed robbery, to be served concurrently. She will be eligible for parole in ten years.

You're the Investigator

1. Describe behavioral traits in Harvey's relationship with authority figures that would lead to her criminal conduct.

_____

_____

_____

_____

_____

_____

_____

_____

_____

_____

2. Discuss the reasons Harvey's relationship with Ketchum contributed to her behavior problems and violent actions against her grandparents.

_____

_____

_____

_____

_____

_____

_____

_____

_____

_____

3. Describe the factors in both Harvey's and Ketchum's child-hood that would lead to their friendship and ultimate relationship.

_____

_____

_____

_____

_____

_____

_____

_____

_____

_____

4. Identify and discuss the motives for Harvey and Ketchum killing Carl and Sarah Collier.

_____

_____

_____

_____

_____

_____

_____

_____

_____

_____

_____

5. Describe what evidence authorities possessed that resulted in the arrest warrants being issued against Harvey and Ketchum.

_____

_____

_____

_____

_____

_____

_____

_____

_____

_____

_____

6. Describe the evidence authorities seized after Harvey's and Ketchum's arrest that would be critical to their successful prosecution.

_____

_____

_____

_____

_____

_____

_____

_____

_____

7. Discuss the relevance of DNA blood analysis on the clothing and knives seized from the truck driven by Harvey and Ketchum.

_____

_____

_____

_____

_____

_____

_____

_____

_____

_____

8. List and describe what circumstances you believe existed that justified authorities charging Harvey and Ketchum as adults.

_____

_____

_____

_____

_____

_____

_____

_____

_____

_____

_____

9. Explain why Ketchum and Harvey were charged with felony murder.

_____

_____

_____

_____

_____

_____

_____

_____

_____

_____

_____

10. Compare and contrast the sentences given to Harvey and Ketchum and discuss why Ketchum would be eligible for parole after serving only a ten-year sentence.

_____

_____

_____

_____

_____

_____

_____

_____

_____

_____

_____

CHAPTER 6

The Amy Fisher Story

Amy Fisher, known as the "Long Island Lolita," was a 17-year-old woman who had anything but a normal childhood. Although Fisher enjoyed an excellent and loving relationship with her mother, Fisher's relationship with her father was dysfunctional. According to Fisher, she tried to avoid her father during her youth because she was terrified of him. In fact, it has been suggested that Amy Fisher's relationship with her father impacted and significantly influenced her later relationship with men, particularly men considerably older than Fisher.

Fisher suffered through several traumatic situations during her youth. Fisher told authorities that she was sexually abused numerous times by a member of her family and that at 13 years of age she was raped in her parent's home by a contractor who was making repairs at the Fisher residence. In addition, while in her teens, Fisher became pregnant by one of her boyfriends and subsequently had an abortion.

Although Fisher had a traumatic childhood, her life took a turn for the worse after she accidentally broke the rearview mirror off her car while backing out of the garage of her home. Concerned about her father's reaction, Fisher decided to take the car to a body shop to repair the mirror so that her father would not know what had happened. On arriving at Complete

Auto Body and Fender Inc., Fisher was told by the owner, Joey Buttafuoco, that the damage to the car would require extensive repair work and would be more expensive than Fisher could afford. To keep Fisher from getting into trouble with her father, Buttafuoco recommended that the teenager tell her father the car was hit by another vehicle while parked. Fearful of her father's reaction if she told the truth, Fisher took Joey's advice.

The Crime

During the next several months, Fisher made numerous trips to the repair shop and began to develop an attraction for the body shop owner, Joey Buttafuoco, who at 35 years of age was more than 18 years older than Fisher. On one visit to the repair shop, Fisher had to leave the car overnight at the shop. Buttafuoco offered to take Fisher home, and on arriving at her parent's home, Buttafuoco made "physical advances towards her in the bedroom," according to Fisher. After this session, Fisher and Buttafuoco's relationship began to flourish, with frequent trips to area hotels. As they grew closer, Buttafuoco opened up to Fisher, telling her how unhappy he was with his wife.

Within two weeks of the beginning of their relationship, Fisher discovered she had herpes. Fisher reluctantly told her parents that she had the viral disease, but she denied it was from Buttafuoco because she feared her parents might try to have him arrested for statutory rape.

During the late summer of 1991, Amy Fisher got a job as a salesperson at a clothing store. Within a month, Fisher was fired from the job. Fisher was desperate for money because she had just purchased a new car. According to Amy, Buttafuoco recommended that she work for an escort service where she could make money quickly. By the end of September 1991, Amy Fisher was making money as a prostitute. Her relationship with Buttafuoco continued, and Fisher began putting pressure on Buttafuoco to leave his wife. Finally, in November 1991, Fisher told Buttafuoco he had to choose between her and his wife. When Buttafuoco refused to leave his wife, Fisher ended their relationship.

It was a difficult period for Fisher, who reportedly even attempted suicide by cutting her wrists. Even though she and Buttafuoco were not seeing each other, she maintained strong feelings for him and became increasingly jealous of Buttafuoco's wife, Mary Jo. At one point, Fisher even posed as a door-to-door salesperson so that she could see Joey Buttafuoco's wife.

During January 1992, Fisher and Buttafuoco began seeing each other again. This time, Fisher was determined not to lose Buttafuoco.

In May 1992, Amy Fisher went to a hair salon where a friend worked. While having her hair styled, Fisher's friend described how her boyfriend was cheating and that she would like to get a gun and shoot the other girl. Fisher's hairdresser's comment resulted in Fisher asking the hairdresser whether she knew where Fisher might obtain a gun. This casual conversation became the first step in Amy Fisher's effort to get rid of Mary Jo Buttafuoco. The hairdresser told Amy that Peter Guagenti would likely be able to find a gun for Fisher.

Amy Fisher later told authorities that she discussed her plan to kill Mary Jo with Joey Buttafuoco. Fisher also alleged that after telling Joey about the plan, he assisted her by telling her how to kill his wife. In preparation to carry out the murder of Mary Jo Buttafuoco, Amy Fisher and Peter Guagenti obtained stolen license plates and put them on Peter Guagenti's car. Then, on May 19, 1992, Peter drove Amy Fisher to the Buttafuoco residence and while en route handed Amy Fisher a .25-caliber semiautomatic pistol that was hidden in his glove compartment.

On arriving at the Buttafuoco residence, Peter Guagenti remained in the parked car while Amy Fisher approached Buttafuoco's front door. As Mary Jo Buttafuoco opened her front door, she observed a teenage girl with long brown hair who asked whether she was Joey Buttafuoco's wife. Mary Jo asked Fisher what she wanted, and Fisher responded by saying that Joey Buttafuoco was having an affair with her 16-year-old sister. During their conversation, Mary Jo noticed Peter Guagenti's parked car in front of the house, and she asked Amy Fisher who he was. Fisher responded that it was her boyfriend. Fisher then told Mary Jo that she could prove that Joey was having an affair with her sister and produced a

T-shirt with the words "Complete Auto Body and Fender, Inc." that Fisher said was given to her sister by Joey.

Mary Jo Buttafuoco became agitated by the accusations about her husband and demanded that Fisher leave. As Mary Jo turned to go back into the house, Fisher hit her in the head with the gun and then shot Mary Jo Buttafuoco in the head at point-blank range.

Hearing the shots, several neighbors ran toward the Buttafuoco residence, where they observed Mary Jo's body on the front porch in a pool of blood. Neighbors immediately called an ambulance that arrived within minutes to transport the seriously injured woman to the hospital.

The Investigation

Police arrived at the scene and immediately began an investigation. The crime scene was unusual because there was no apparent evidence that it was a robbery and highly unlikely that a house wife would be the target of an organized-crime shooting.

By the time Mary Jo Buttafuoco arrived at the hospital, her condition was grave, and because the severity of the wounds, she was given little chance for survival. After several hours in the operating room, doctors were able to improve Mary Jo's condition ever so slightly. However, surgeons were unable to remove the bullet from her head, and Mary Jo's condition remained critical.

While Mary Jo Buttafuoco was undergoing surgery, her husband, Joey, was being interviewed by police, who were desperately trying to determine why the housewife was shot in the doorway to her home. Joey Buttafuoco told police that it was possible that a girl named Amy and her boyfriend might have sought revenge against Joey because he recommended to Amy that she not loan him money to pay off a drug debt. Detectives were suspicious of Joey's story but at that point had no other significant leads.

On May 20, 1992, Mary Jo regained consciousness, and investigators immediately went to the hospital to interview her. Mary Jo remembered a number of important details, including a description of the teenage girl, a description of the car occupied by who she thought was the girl's boyfriend, and information about the T-shirt from Joey Buttafuoco's business. Shortly after the interview with Mary Jo, Joey Buttafuoco told investigators who he thought might have shot his wife and gave Amy Fisher's name to the officers.

Detectives obtained a photograph of Amy Fisher, who was subsequently identified by Mary Jo as the girl who shot her. On the basis of the positive photo identification, authorities obtained an arrest warrant for Amy Fisher.

On May 21, 1992, police arrested Amy Fisher at her home after Joey Buttafuoco agreed to call Amy's house to see if she was there. Shortly after her capture, Amy Fisher found out that Joey was responsible for her arrest. Amy admitted to police that she was at Mary Jo's house but said the gun discharged accidentally. Amy also told investigators that she had an affair with Joey and that it was Joey who gave her the gun.

When Joey was interviewed by detectives on May 22, 1992, he denied giving the weapon to Amy Fisher. Although Joey knew police had no evidence that he was involved in his wife's shooting, Joey was concerned that information was known to police about his affair with Amy Fisher.

The Trial

On May 29, Amy Fisher was indicted by the grand jury in Nassau County for attempted murder, armed felony, assault, and several other offenses. Amy's bail was set at $2 million.

Fisher's attorney began a plea-bargaining process with the Nassau County District Attorney's office in which Amy would accept a sentence of between 5 and 15 years in prison and in return would agree to testify against Joey Buttafuoco. At her December sentencing hearing, Amy Fisher was given a 15-year prison sentence, and in February, Peter Guagenti, who supplied the gun and drove her to the scene, received a six-month jail sentence.

When Amy Fisher was sentenced to prison and no charges were brought against Joey Buttafuoco, Joey thought he was absolved of any criminal conduct. However, in February 1993, the district attorney in Nassau County decided to reopen the case against Joey Buttafuoco based on his sexual misconduct with Amy Fisher. Fisher, who was only 16 years of age, alleged that Buttafuoco had sex with her in various hotels. Later in the spring of 1993, Fisher was taken from her prison cell and placed before a grand jury investigating Joey Buttafuoco. Amy Fisher testified that Buttafuoco had engaged in sexual relations with her on numerous occasions beginning when she was only 16 years of age. Grand jury evidence included hotel receipts showing that Joey had paid for hotel rooms. Mary Jo Buttafuoco testified before the grand jury that her husband had not cheated on her and that Amy Fisher was a liar. But despite his wife's testimony, Joey was indicted for rape, sodomy, and endangering the welfare of a child. Joey Buttafuoco pled not guilty to the charges.

During the months that followed, prosecutors built a strong case against Joey Buttafuoco, ultimately resulting in Joey changing his plea to guilty. In October 1993, Buttafuoco was convicted of one count of statutory rape and spent six months in jail for his crime.

After Buttafuoco completed his jail sentence, he moved to California, where he was arrested for soliciting sex from an undercover police officer. In 2004, Joey was arrested again for his involvement in an illegal auto-insurance scheme.

The Buttafuoco's marriage ended in the spring of 2003 when Joey and Mary Jo agreed to a divorce.

Amy Fisher was released from prison after serving seven years of her 15-year sentence. She remained on parole status until 2003. Several years after her release from prison, Amy Fisher married a man more than 20 years her senior, and they reside in the New York area with their young son.

You're the Investigator

1. Describe the factors in Amy Fisher's childhood that may have caused her delinquent behavior as a teenager.

   _____

   _____

   _____

   _____

_____

_____

_____

_____

_____

_____

_____

_____

2. Discuss the meaning of the term *statutory rape* in legal terms. What is the comparable offense in the jurisdiction in which you reside?

_____

_____

_____

_____

_____

_____

_____

_____

_____

_____

_____

3. Discuss the school or social service programs you believe could have helped Amy Fisher during her teenage years.

_____

_____

_____

_____

_____

_____

_____

_____

_____

_____

_____

4. Describe the conversation Amy Fisher had that resulted in her obtaining a handgun to shoot Mary Jo Buttafuoco and why she made the decision to shoot Mary Jo.

_____

_____

_____

_____

_____

_____

_____

_____

_____

_____

5. List and discuss the evidence that authorities obtained during the Amy Fisher investigation.

_____

_____

_____

_____

_____

_____

_____

_____

_____

_____

_____

6. Do you think Amy Fisher is a ruthless young woman or a victim herself?

_____

_____

_____

_____

_____

_____

_____

_____

_____

_____

7. Identify and explain what you believe to be the most important piece of information that Mary Jo Buttafuoco provided to authorities that led to Amy Fisher's arrest.

_____

_____

_____

_____

_____

_____

_____

_____

_____

_____

_____

8. Discuss what a grand jury indictment means in our legal system.

_____

_____

_____

_____

_____

_____

_____

_____

_____

_____

_____

9. Describe the evidence authorities possessed to convict Joey Buttafuoco of statutory rape.

_____

_____

_____

_____

_____

_____

_____

_____

_____

_____

_____

10. Justify why you believe or do not believe that the sentences given to Amy Fisher and Joey Buttafuoco were sufficient.

_____

_____

_____

_____

_____

_____

_____

_____

_____

_____

_____

_____

CHAPTER 7

The James Bulger Abduction

On February 12, 1993, Denise Bulger, the mother of three-year-old James, went shopping with her brother's girlfriend at the Bootie Strand Shopping Center near Liverpool, England. James was Denise Bulger's only child, and she was cautious about not letting him out of her sight. It was about 2:30 P.M. when the two women with their children in tow entered the mall.

After shopping at several stores, the children were becoming restless, but Denise Bulger had one more stop to make at the butcher shop. Denise entered the store, leaving her son, James, near the front door to play. Within a few moments, Denise completed her shopping and headed to the door to get her child when she realized the three-year-old was gone. She frantically searched around the area of the store's entrance and then ran back inside the store and cried out that her infant son was missing. Security personnel were immediately notified, and police were summoned.

The Crime

Earlier that same morning, ten-year-old Jon Venables and Robert Thompson prepared to leave home for school. The boys' chance meeting on the way to school resulted in them deciding to skip classes and have some fun. Both Jon and Robert frequently skipped school, and both boys had been held back a grade because of problems they encountered in school.

Jon and Robert decided to go to the Bootie Strand Shopping Center and shoplift; it was like a game to the boys. They strolled through several stores, putting various items in their pockets while the clerks were busy with other customers. They stole batteries, paint, a doll, candy, and other trinkets. Their horseplay got out of hand when they began tormenting an elderly woman and then ran off after they punched the woman in her back.

As the day went on, the boys became more daring. At some point, Robert would later tell authorities, Jon suggested that they should "get a kid." With the boys now focused on impressing each other, they decided to find a child.

Jon and Robert entered the TJ Hughes department store, where they encountered a three-year-old girl and her two-year-old brother who were shopping with their mother. While the woman was paying for several items she purchased, Jon and Robert lured the baby boy out of the store. As the mother turned to find her children, she realized her son was gone. The woman's daughter told her that her brother went with some boys. The mother ran out of the store looking for her son and observed two boys coaxing her son to follow them. The mother hollered her child's name, and at that point, Jon and Robert quickly left the area, letting the little boy return to his mother.

Robert and Jon then headed for a candy store that was located near the butcher shop. As the boys approached, they noticed a small boy standing by the door of the butcher shop. Jon and Robert called to the boy to come to them. At 3:42 P.M., the mall security camera recorded Jon, Robert, and the toddler walking out of the mall.

As the boys walked away from the mall, their captive, young James Bulger, began crying for his mother. Ignoring the child's screams, Jon and Robert held the little boy's hand as they walked to a canal in a secluded area. Both boys joked about throwing the child into the canal. Although they did not throw the boy in the canal, it was at this location that the boys initially injured James Bulger. One of the boys picked James up and dropped him on his head, causing a laceration and severe bruising.

A woman walking near the canal saw the child with the boys but assumed they were playing. Jon and Robert quickly covered James with a hood in an attempt to hide his injuries. Jon, Robert, and young James then walked aimlessly past several shopping areas where they were observed by several motorists swinging the boy by his arms and dragging the crying child down the street. One motorist later told authorities he observed Robert kick the baby in his ribs. The child broke loose from the boys and ran into the street but was caught by the boys, who then carried the child to a reservoir area.

While at the reservoir, a woman who noticed the baby approached the boys and inquired why the baby was crying. Jon and Robert responded that they just found the boy nearby and didn't know the child. The elderly lady told the boys to take the child to the local police station, which was only a few blocks away. The woman gave the boys directions to get to the police station but then stood by as the boys headed off with the child in the opposite direction of the police station.

Several hours later, the elderly woman saw a news report on television about the missing child and immediately contacted police to report her encounter with the boys. She told authorities she regretted not doing something to help the child.

As the boys continued walking with young James, they encountered another woman on the street who noticed that James was injured. She also asked Jon and Robert what was wrong with the child. The boys responded by telling the lady that they found the boy at the mall and were taking him to the police station. Another concerned passerby, with her young daughter, approached as the boys were explaining how they got the boy. She also questioned the boys, who seemed quite nervous. Robert offered to hand James over to the woman when Jon took the boy by the hand and said they were taking him to the police station. The woman with the young daughter was suspicious and asked the other woman if she would watch her daughter while she went with the boys to ensure that the child got to the police station. The other woman refused to watch the girl, and at that point, the boys took off with young James.

Jon and Robert continued walking with the injured child, and as authorities would later determine, more than 30 other witnesses saw the young boy with Jon and Robert during their several-hour ordeal. Although they took no action, many witnesses recognized that the child was suffering from injuries. Not knowing what to do with the boy and with evening approaching, Jon and Robert decided to go to the railroad tracks, where their final assault and murder of James Bulger would occur. It was nearing 6:00 P.M. when one of the boys threw paint at James's face. The paint went into the little boy's eye, and he began to scream. The boys then began pelting the child with rocks and kicking him. The boys then took James's shoes off along with his pants and hit young James with a large metal bar. Believing that James was dead, Jon and Robert placed the child's lifeless body across the railroad tracks and covered his bloody head with rocks. Jon and Robert left the scene and headed home.

The Investigation

Young James Bulger's disappearance was widely publicized on the evening news. Many listeners, believing they had seen James, began calling in information to authorities.

As is normal in child abduction cases, parents are considered potential suspects by authorities until they can be eliminated from suspicion. Authorities interviewed Denise Bulger and her husband Ralph in order to determine exactly what happened prior to and during James's disappearance. On the basis of the number of other leads police had and the number of witnesses who saw James with Jon and Robert, authorities were certain the parents were not involved in James's disappearance.

When investigators reviewed the surveillance video from the mall, they immediately realized they were not dealing with adults but rather with two young boys. The quality of the video was not good enough to positively identify the boys, but it clearly showed James being led away from the mall by two other children.

Police conducted an intensive manhunt to find the child. Searchers were organized to look for the child throughout the area near the mall where the boy was last seen. Even an underwater search was conducted in the canal to see whether the young child's body could be found. Police also released photos from the mall video to the public to determine whether anyone could recognize the two boys who took James Bulger from the shopping center.

On Sunday afternoon, following James Bulger's disappearance, boys playing in the area of the railroad tracks discovered James Bulger's body. The boys contacted the police, who immediately responded and established a crime-scene perimeter. As police investigated, it was determined that a train had severed James Bulger's torso, with his upper torso located some distance from the rest of his body. The crime scene investigation revealed that the child's waist had been placed across the track. Police also found a bloody iron bar, approximately 2 feet long, along with numerous bricks and rocks that contained blood. The forensic examination of James's body revealed that he suffered numerous severe blows to the head and upper body as well as a deep bruise that contained a shoe imprint on the child's cheek. Although there was no positive evidence of a sexual assault, authorities believed that some of the injuries the child suffered below his waist were consistent with sexual abuse.

Police decided that both boys should be interviewed. Authorities obtained warrants and arrested both boys and searched their homes. Both boys began to cry when they realized they were suspects. Police found blood on Robert's shoes that would later be traced to the crime scene. When Jon was arrested, police seized his mustard-colored jacket, which had blue paint on it consistent with the paint found on little James Bulger.

When police began questioning both of the boys, the parents and a legal representative were permitted to be present because of the boys' age. Authorities separated both boys during questioning and attempted to determine whether the boys understood their legal rights and knew the difference between telling the truth and lying.

During the interviews, Robert admitted that both boys were at the mall and even told authorities that he remembered seeing James Bulger and his mother. Jon, on the other hand, admitted he was with Robert but denied going to the mall. But it was Robert who became sarcastic with investigators and continually denied having any contact with James Bulger.

As authorities continued interviewing and putting more pressure on both boys, Robert spontaneously said it was Jon's picture in the paper holding the boy by his hand. Robert opened up even more when police told him he would be held overnight and could not go home. Robert then blurted out defiantly, "Why do I have to stay here? Jon's the one that took the baby."

After several more hours of questioning, Robert's mother urged him to tell the truth. At that point, Robert claimed it was Jon who threw a brick at James Bulger's face and hit him with a heavy metal bar. Robert continued to put all the blame on Jon and would not admit to any role in hurting James.

Jon, on the other hand, continued to cry hysterically during most of his interview, denying any involvement in hurting the boy. It was obvious that Jon was holding back, and at that point both his mother and his father reassured Jon they would love him regardless of what he had done. Both parents then urged Jon to tell the truth. Jon began to cry and stated that he was involved in young James Bulger's death. As Jon began to describe what happened, he put most of the blame on Robert, indicating that Robert threw the paint in the young child's face and also hit the child in the head with a brick. Jon even claimed he tried to stop Robert from throwing bricks at the child's head.

Authorities finally believed they had obtained sufficient evidence to charge both boys with James Bulger's murder and the attempted abduction of the other child at the mall. Both boys were detained pending their trial, which was scheduled for November 1993. In the interim, the courts in England had to determine how and where to confine the two boys because of their age. Authorities also ordered the boys to undergo extensive psychiatric examination in preparation for their trial. The results of both boys' psychiatric exams indicated that neither boy suffered from mental illness, that both possessed average intelligence, and that the boys recognized that when someone was killed, they could not be brought back to life.

The Trial

While both boys awaited their trial, they were given fictitious identities for their own safety. They were also held in a special, secure detention facility and separated from each other.

Because of their small stature, special arrangements were made in the courtroom to elevate the platform on which the two boys would sit in order for them to observe the proceedings. When the trial began, the prosecution presented its case first, indicating that both boys were responsible for James Bulger's death. The prosecution argued that both boys knew that their action of taking the boy from his mother was wrong and that it was equally wrong for them to use the level of violence on the boy that led to his death.

The prosecution presented physical and forensic evidence that placed the boys at the scene of James Bulger's murder. Evidence included mall security videos, blue paint on their clothing and on the child, bloody bricks at the scene, and Robert's bloody shoe imprint on James Bulger's cheek.

Psychiatric testimony presented by the prosecution established that both boys knew the seriousness of their actions and that they understood the nature of the crimes for which they were charged.

In his closing arguments, the prosecutor argued that despite the two boys pointing the finger at each other as being responsible for James Bulger's death, both boys were together when James sustained his injuries and therefore are equally liable for his death.

After the prosecution rested its case, the defense argued that neither boy had been involved in any violent behavior before. The defense argued that the boys committed a prank and had no intention of killing the child. The defense argued that the boys became frightened and didn't know what to do with James, so they went home and left him near the railroad tracks. Neither of the boys testified in his own defense.

After nearly a three-week trial, the case went to the jury. The jury returned its verdict later that same afternoon, and both Jon Venables and Robert Thompson were found guilty of murdering James Bulger.

In sentencing the boys, the judge said, "Killing James Bulger was an act of unparalleled evil and barbarity. . . . In my judgment your conduct was both cunning and very wicked."

The boys were sentenced to 15 years in detention and were detained at separate secret locations in the north of England. An appeal was filed on the boys' behalf, arguing that ten-year-old boys should never have been tried as adults. On June 22, 2001, after serving an eight-year sentence, the British Parole Board agreed to release both boys.

You're the Investigator

1. Analyze why various witnesses to James Bulger's abduction did little or nothing to assist the boy.

   _____

   _____

   _____

   _____

   _____

   _____

   _____

   _____

   _____

   _____

   _____

2. Discuss why you believe or don't believe a witness has a responsibility to report criminal conduct to police.

   _____

   _____

   _____

   _____

   _____

   _____

   _____

_____

_____

_____

_____

3. Analyze why police routinely consider parents as potential suspects in child abduction cases.

_____

_____

_____

_____

_____

_____

_____

_____

_____

_____

_____

4. Describe what you think Jon's and Robert's motive was in abducting James Bulger.

_____

_____

_____

_____

_____

_____

_____

_____

_____

_____

_____

_____

5. Analyze and discuss the evidence that enabled police to identify James Bulger's abductors.

_____

_____

_____

_____

_____

_____

_____

_____

_____

_____

_____

6. Discuss the evidence seized during Jon's and Robert's arrest at their homes.

_____

_____

_____

_____

_____

_____

_____

_____

_____

_____

_____

7. Describe and discuss the rationale for separating Jon and Robert during questioning and permitting their parents to participate in police interviews of the boys.

_____

_____

_____

_____

_____

_____

_____

_____

_____

_____

_____

8. Discuss the reasons why a psychiatric examination was conducted of Jon and Robert prior to their trial.

_____

_____

_____

_____

_____

_____

_____

_____

_____

_____

_____

9. Describe what you believe to be the most compelling evidence presented by prosecutors against Jon and Robert.

_____

_____

_____

_____

_____

_____

_____

_____

_____

_____

_____

10. Discuss your opinion as to the fairness of the trial court's original sentence of the boys and the arguments to the parole board to release the boys prior to completing their sentence.

_____

_____

_____

_____

_____

_____

_____

_____

_____

_____

_____